C000312117

Published by Ice House Books

Editor: Zulekhá Afzal
Designer: Kayleigh Hudson
Photography credits overleaf

Ice House Books is an imprint of Half Moon Bay Limited
The Ice House, 124 Walcot Street, Bath, BA1 5BG
www.icehousebooks.co.uk

ISBN 978-1-912867-91-2

Printed in China

Vegan Wizardry

ICE HOUSE BOOKS

p9 Timolina / shutterstock.com
p11 MariaKovaleva / shutterstock.com
p13 Brent Hofacker / shutterstock.com
p15 Nataliya Arzamasova / shutterstock.com
p17 Lucky_elephant / shutterstock.com
p19 mmkarabella / shutterstock.com
p21 JeniFoto / shutterstock.com
p23 Larisa Blinova / shutterstock.com
p25 Anna Kurzaeva / shutterstock.com
p29 YuliiaHolovchenko / shutterstock.com
p33 zarzamora / shutterstock.com
p35 sarsmis / shutterstock.com
p39 Nataliya Arzamasova / shutterstock.com
p43 Kiian Oksana / shutterstock.com
p47 Nataliya Arzamasova / shutterstock.com
p49 Chudovska / shutterstock.com
p53 vm2002 / shutterstock.com
p57 Kalinka Georgieva / shutterstock.com
p59 viennetta / shutterstock.com
p61 NoirChocolate / shutterstock.com

Contents

Sunset Skies (Beetroot Hummus)

Ingredients

- 250 g (9 oz) beetroot
- 2x 400 g (28 oz) tin chickpeas, drained and rinsed. Reserve the aquafaba (chickpea water) and several chickpeas for garnish
- 2 garlic cloves, minced
- 2 tbsp tahini
- salt
- 4 tbsp lemon juice
- extra virgin olive oil for garnish
- parsley for garnish, roughly chopped
- salad leaves for garnish
- sesame seeds for garnish

Makes: several servings
Prep Time: 15 to 20 minutes
Cook Time: 60 minutes

Method

1. Preheat the oven to 200°C/180°C fan/Gas 6.
2. To bake the beetroots, place them in the middle of some tin foil. Hold up the foil edges and drizzle some water over the beetroots so they can cook in their own steam, then scrunch up the foil to create a parcel. Pop the parcel on a baking tray and bake for approx. 60 minutes until you can pierce the beetroots. Peel the beetroots once cool.
3. Slice the beetroots and add them to a blender, along with the chickpeas, minced garlic, tahini, salt and lemon juice. Pour in some of the aquafaba and blend until smooth and creamy. If it's too thick, continue adding small amounts of aquafaba until it reaches the desired consistency.
4. Serve and garnish with a drizzle of oil, chopped parsley, some salad leaves, chickpeas and sesame seeds. Enjoy with toasted pitta or pitta chips.

Ghostly Secrets (*Cashew Mayonnaise*)

Ingredients

- 250 g (9 oz) cashews, soaked
- 300 ml (10 fl oz) water, plus extra to soak cashews
- 1 garlic clove, minced
- salt
- basil for garnish

Makes: several servings
Prep Time: 5 to 10 minutes
Extra Time: 2 hours

Method

1. Put the cashews in a bowl and cover them with water. Leave to soak for approx. two hours until softened. Drain and rinse well.
2. Add all the ingredients to a blender and purée until smooth and creamy.
3. Serve as a dip and garnish with a sprig of basil. Alternatively, add a little more water to the blender and blitz again to make a sauce suitable for pasta or salad dishes.

BUBBLING BROTH
(Butternut Squash Soup)

INGREDIENTS

Makes: 3 to 4 servings
Prep Time: 10 to 15 minutes
Cook Time: 50 minutes

- 1 tbsp olive oil
- 1 white onion, finely chopped
- 1 garlic clove, finely chopped
- 1 celery stalk, chopped
- 1 carrot, chopped
- ½ a butternut squash, peeled, deseeded and chopped
- 475 ml (16 fl oz) vegetable stock
- 120 ml (4 fl oz) unsweetened soya milk
- salt and pepper
- butternut squash or pumpkin seeds for garnish
- sage leaves for garnish

Method

1. Heat the oil in a large pan over a medium heat and add the onion, garlic and celery. Stir often and sauté until softened (approximately five minutes).
2. Add the carrot and butternut squash then pour in the vegetable stock. Bring to the boil then reduce to a simmer. Leave the vegetables to cook for approx. 30–40 minutes, until tender.
3. Transfer the broth to a blender and blend until smooth (this step may have to be completed in a few batches). Once blended, transfer the soup back to the large pan.
4. Pour in the soya milk and season to taste with salt and pepper, stirring well.
5. Once it's warmed through, serve the soup with the seeds and sage leaves on top. Enjoy with warmed or toasted bread.

Bewitched (Green Pea Soup)

Ingredients

- 1 tbsp olive oil
- 1 white onion, finely chopped
- 1 garlic clove, finely chopped
- 1 large potato, peeled and diced
- 300 g (10 oz) peas, plus blanched peas for garnish
- 700 ml (24 fl oz) vegetable stock
- salt and pepper
- parsley, roughly chopped
- 1 tbsp lemon juice
- mint for garnish

Makes: 3 to 4 servings
Prep Time: 15 minutes
Cook Time: 20 to 25 minutes

Method

1. Heat the oil in a large pan over a medium heat. Once hot, add the onion and garlic and gently fry them until translucent.
2. Add the potato, peas, vegetable stock, salt and pepper, and parsley. Stir and turn the heat down to low. Leave to simmer for approximately 15 minutes or until the diced potato and peas are tender.
3. Remove the pan from the heat and stir in the lemon juice.

4. Transfer the broth to a blender and blend until smooth (this step may have to be completed in a few batches).
5. Prepare the blanched peas for garnish by heating some water in a pan. Once boiling, add two handfuls of peas and leave them to cook for one minute. Have a bowl of ice-cold water ready. Remove the peas from the boiling water and transfer them to the bowl of cold water. Leave them to cool for five minutes, then drain.
6. Warm the soup through in a pan and garnish with the blanched peas and mint.

Wizard's Blood (Tomato Soup)

Ingredients

- 1 tbsp coconut oil
- 1 white onion, finely chopped
- 1 garlic clove, finely chopped
- 1 tsp oregano
- 1 tsp dried basil
- 400 g (14 oz) tin tomatoes
- 2 tbsp brown sugar
- 2 large potatoes, peeled and diced
- 475 ml (16 fl oz) vegetable stock
- basil for garnish
- freshly ground black pepper for garnish

Makes: 3 to 4 servings
Prep Time: 10 to 15 minutes
Cook Time: 40 minutes

Method

1. Heat the oil in a pan over a medium heat. Once the oil is hot, add the onion and garlic and sauté. After 1–2 minutes, add the oregano and basil and continue to sauté until the onion has softened.

2 Stir in the tin of tomatoes and sugar, then add the potatoes. Pour in the vegetable stock and give the ingredients another good stir.

3 Bring to the boil then reduce to a simmer for approximately 30 minutes, until the vegetables have softened.

4 Transfer the broth to a blender and blend until smooth (this step may have to be completed in a few batches).

5 Warm the soup through in the pan then serve with fresh basil and peppercorns to decorate. Tuck in!

Broken Heart (Roasted Cauliflower Steak)

Ingredients

- 3 tbsp olive oil
- 4 garlic cloves, minced
- 1 tsp dried oregano
- ½ tsp dried parsley
- ½ tsp dried thyme
- ½ tsp dried rosemary
- 2 cauliflower heads, cut into ½ inch slices
- salt and pepper

Makes: 4 servings
Prep Time: 15 minutes
Cook Time: 25 minutes

Method

1. Preheat the oven to 200°C/180°C fan/Gas 6 and lightly oil a baking sheet.
2. Add the remaining oil, garlic and herbs to a small bowl and mix them together.
3. Lay the cauliflower heads out on the baking sheet and lightly brush both sides with the oil mixture. Season with salt and pepper.

4 Bake for approximately 20–25 minutes or until they are golden brown. Flip the cauliflower heads halfway through baking.

5 Serve hot with a selection of your favourite roasted or steamed veggies.

Mermaid's Hair (Butternut Squash Noodles)

Ingredients

- ½ a butternut squash, peeled and deseeded
- 2 tbsp olive oil
- salt and pepper
- 1 garlic clove, minced
- 50 g (2 oz) mushrooms, sliced
- 200 g (7 oz) spinach
- butternut squash or pumpkin seeds for garnish

Makes: 2 servings
Prep Time: 10 to 15 minutes
Cook Time: 10 to 12 minutes

Method

1. Preheat the oven to 200°C/180°C fan/Gas 6.
2. Put the butternut squash through a spiralizer to create noodles. If the noodles are quite long, cut them with clean kitchen scissors to roughly the same length as long pasta.
3. Spread the squash noodles out on a baking tray and drizzle over ½–1 tablespoon of oil, then season well with salt and pepper. Toss the noodles so they're all coated.
4. Bake for approx. 10–12 minutes until tender. Be careful not to overcook the noodles – you don't want them to be crispy.
5. While the noodles are in the oven, heat one tablespoon of oil in a pan. Add the garlic and mushrooms and cook until softened. Add the spinach and continue to cook until it's wilted.
6. When everything is cooked, toss the ingredients together until combined, then serve. Garnish with the seeds and enjoy.

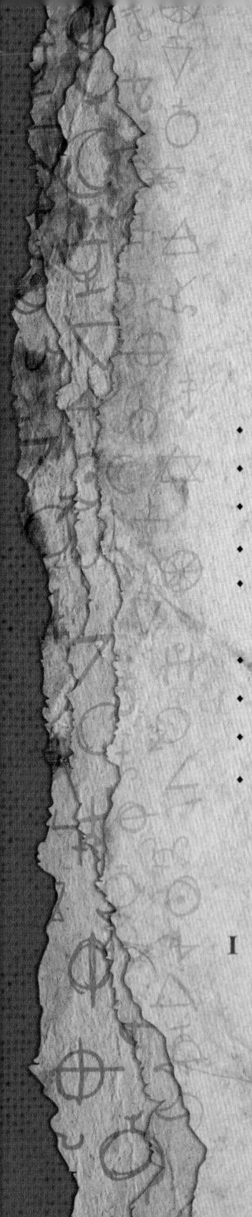

Avo-cadabra! (Avocado Pesto Pasta)

Ingredients

For the avocado pesto:

- 1 ripe avocado
- 2 garlic cloves, chopped
- 2 small handfuls parsley
- small handful basil
- 25 g (1 oz) roasted salted pistachios
- 4 tbsp lemon juice
- 1 tbsp nutritional yeast
- 1 tbsp olive oil
- salt and pepper

For the pasta:

- 285 g (10 oz) vegan tortiglioni, or your favourite pasta
- salt

Makes: 4 servings
Prep Time: 10 minutes
Cook Time: 15 minutes

Method

1 Begin by making the avocado pesto. Cut the avocado in half by running a knife around it from top to bottom. Twist the avocado in half and take out the pit. Use a spoon to remove the flesh, then discard the skin and pit.

2. Put the avocado flesh into a blender, along with the other pesto ingredients, and blend until smooth.
3. Bring a pan of salted water to the boil over a medium heat and cook your pasta according to the packet instructions. Once cooked, drain well then return the pasta to the pan.
4. Add the pesto to the pan (as much as you like) and gently stir until the pasta is covered. (Any leftover pesto can be stored in a covered bowl or jar in the fridge.) Serve warm.

Mythical Gems (*Pumpkin Macaroni 'Cheese'*)

Ingredients

- 75 g (3 oz) cashews, soaked
- 450 g (16 oz) vegan cavatappi, or your favourite pasta
- 2 tbsp extra virgin olive oil
- 2 shallots, diced
- 3 garlic cloves, chopped
- 425 g (15 oz) pumpkin purée
- 1 tsp vegetable bouillon
- 250 ml (9 fl oz) reserved pasta water
- 1 tbsp nutritional yeast
- 1 tbsp white vinegar
- 1 tsp smoked paprika
- 1 tsp dried sage
- salt and pepper
- parsley for garnish, roughly chopped

Makes: 4 servings
Prep Time: 15 minutes
Extra time: 30 minutes
Cook Time: 30 minutes

Turn the page for the method.

Method

1. Begin by soaking the cashews in boiled water for 30 minutes. Once soaked, drain and rinse them well.
2. Bring a large pan of salted water to the boil and cook the pasta according to the packet instructions. Once cooked, drain the pasta – reserving 250 ml (9 fl oz) of the pasta water – and return the pasta to the pan.
3. While the pasta is cooking, heat the oil in a large pan over a medium heat. Add the shallots and cook them until translucent (approximately 2–3 minutes). Stir in the garlic and cook for another two minutes, then remove the pan from the heat.
4. Put the drained cashews, cooked shallots and garlic, reserved pasta water and remaining ingredients into a blender (except the parsley for garnish). Blend on high until smooth and creamy.
5. Pour the pumpkin sauce over the pasta. Warm the mac and 'cheese' over a medium heat, stirring well so all the pasta is covered with the sauce. Cook until heated through.
6. Serve with a sprinkling of parsley on top.

Summer Sorcery (*Falafel Sandwich*)

Ingredients

For the falafels:

- 400 g (14 oz) tin chickpeas, drained and rinsed
- 1 white onion, minced
- 4 garlic cloves, minced
- small handful parsley, roughly chopped
- small handful sesame seeds
- 1½ tsp cumin
- salt and pepper
- 4 tbsp plain flour
- 2 tbsp avocado oil

For the sandwich:

- bread rolls
- mixed salad leaves
- 1 small red onion, sliced
- 1–2 large tomatoes, sliced

Makes: 12 falafels
Prep Time: 20 minutes
Extra Time: 1 to 2 hours
Cook time: 10 to 15 minutes

Turn the page for the method.

Method

1. Put the chickpeas, onion, garlic, parsley, sesame seeds, cumin, salt and pepper into a blender. Blend until it forms into a crumbly dough, scraping down the sides as necessary.
2. Add the flour, one tablespoon at a time, and continue to mix until the dough is no longer wet. It should be mouldable.
3. Put the dough in a mixing bowl, cover it and pop it in the fridge to chill and firm up for 1–2 hours.
4. Once it's chilled, spoon out the dough to make 12 falafels (about one heaped tablespoon per falafel). Gently press the dough into small discs.
5. Heat the oil in a large pan on a medium heat. Once hot, arrange as many falafels as will fit in the pan. Cook the falafels, flipping them so both sides turn golden brown, for approximately 4–5 minutes. Repeat this step until all the falafels are cooked.
6. Slice the rolls in half and assemble your sandwiches by layering the salad leaves, red onion and tomato slices. Top with two falafels and enjoy with your favourite vegan sauces!

Forest Disguise (Portobello Mushroom Burger)

Ingredients

Makes: 1 serving
Prep Time: 10 to 15 minutes
Cook Time: 10 minutes

- 2 portobello mushrooms
- drizzle of olive oil
- salt and pepper
- guacamole
- 1 large tomato, sliced
- mixed salad leaves
- vegan mayonnaise
- sesame seeds for garnish

Method

1. Prepare the mushrooms by removing their stalks. Drizzle over some olive oil and season well with salt and pepper.
2. Heat a pan over a medium heat and fry both sides of each mushroom for a few minutes, until they begin to brown. Set them aside to cool a little.

3 Assemble the burger with a helping of guacamole, a thick slice of tomato and salad leaves. Finish with a helping of vegan mayonnaise.

4 Top the burger with the other mushroom half and sprinkle over some sesame seeds for an authentic-looking burger.

Divine Seer
(Beetroot Burger)

Ingredients

For the beetroot patty:

- 250 ml (9 fl oz) balsamic vinegar
- 50 g (2 oz) brown sugar
- 110 g (4 oz) rolled oats
- 400 g (14 oz) tin black beans, drained and rinsed
- 225 g (8 oz) beetroot, grated
- 1 white onion, chopped
- 2 garlic cloves, minced
- sprig of dill, chopped
- salt and pepper
- 1 tbsp rapeseed oil

For the burger:

- bread rolls
- 1 red onion, sliced
- 2 large tomatoes, sliced
- 1 avocado, sliced
- mixed salad leaves

Makes: 6 beetroot patties
Prep Time: 15 to 20 minutes
Cook Time: 30 minutes

Turn the page for the method.

Method

1. Warm the balsamic vinegar and sugar in a small pan over a medium heat. Bring to a simmer then lower the heat and allow the mixture to cook for approx. 15 minutes until it's a thick, syrup consistency. Stir occasionally.
2. Take the pan off the heat and leave the balsamic mixture to cool.
3. Put the oats in a food processor and process until they resemble a coarse powder. Add the black beans, beetroot, onion, garlic, dill, salt and pepper, and two tablespoons of the balsamic mix. Pulse until well combined.
4. Shape the burger mixture into six patties. Heat the oil in a large pan over a medium heat. Arrange as many patties as will fit in the pan, without overcrowding them.
5. Cook the patties until they are lightly browned on both sides (approx. four minutes on each side). Drizzle 1–2 teaspoons of the balsamic mixture over each patty, then flip them and drizzle the other side. Let them cook for a few seconds more before transferring the patties to a plate.
6. Assemble your burgers by layering your salad fillings and a beetroot patty in a bun. Enjoy with your favourite vegan sauces and sides!

Comfort Creations (*Aubergine Balls*)

Ingredients

For the balls:

- 1 tbsp olive oil
- 450 g (16 oz) aubergine, unpeeled and chopped
- salt and pepper
- 60 ml (2 fl oz) water
- 1 white onion, finely chopped
- 2 garlic cloves, minced
- ¼ tsp cayenne pepper
- 400 g (14 oz) tin cannellini beans, drained and rinsed
- small handful parsley, chopped
- red chilli flakes
- 70 g (2 oz) breadcrumbs

For serving:

- white rice
- vegan marinara sauce to drizzle
- parsley for garnish, roughly chopped

Makes: 12 to 16 meatballs
Prep Time: 20 to 30 minutes
Cook Time: 30 to 35 minutes

Turn the page for the method.

Method

1. Preheat the oven to 190°C/ 170°C fan/Gas 5.
2. Heat half a tablespoon of oil in a large pan over a medium heat. Once hot, add the aubergine and season with salt and pepper. Sauté for approximately five minutes.
3. Pour in the water and allow the aubergine to cook for another 10–15 minutes until tender, stirring occasionally. Once the aubergine is cooked, carefully pour the aubergine mixture into a food processor.
4. In the pan, add the remaining half a tablespoon of oil along with the onion, garlic and cayenne pepper. Cook until the onion and garlic have softened and turned translucent. Add them to the aubergine mixture in the food processor, along with the cannellini beans, parsley and chilli flakes.
5. Pulse the ingredients until they're well combined, but be careful not to purée them.
6. Transfer the mixture to a large bowl and stir in the breadcrumbs until combined.
7. Roll the mixture into evenly sized balls and place them on a baking tray. Bake for approximately 30–35 minutes, turning the balls at 15 minutes.
8. While the balls are baking, cook the rice according to the packet instructions and warm through the marinara sauce.
9. Once cooked, serve the aubergine balls over rice with a drizzle of marinara sauce and fresh parsley to garnish.

Mysterious Illusions (Shepherd's Pie)

Ingredients

For the topping:

- 4 large potatoes, peeled and chopped
- 45 g (2 oz) vegan butter
- salt and pepper

Makes: 4 servings
Prep Time: 30 minutes
Extra Time: 30 minutes
Cook Time: 30 minutes

For the filling:

- 1 tbsp olive oil
- 1 white onion, diced
- 2 garlic cloves, minced
- salt and pepper
- 280 g (10 oz) uncooked brown lentils, rinsed and drained
- 1 tsp thyme
- 1 tsp parsley, roughly chopped
- 920 ml (32 fl oz) vegetable stock
- 280 g (10 oz) mixed frozen vegetables (such as peas, carrots and sweetcorn)

Turn the page for the method.

Method

1. Put your chopped potatoes into a large pan and cover them with water. Add a pinch of salt and bring the pan to the boil, then reduce to a simmer. Cover and leave to cook for approximately 20–30 minutes, until tender.
2. While the potatoes are cooking, preheat the oven to 220°C/200°C fan/Gas 7 and lightly grease your baking dish.
3. Heat the oil in a large pan over a medium heat and add the onion and garlic. Sauté for approx. five minutes until lightly browned, and season well.
4. Stir in the lentils and herbs, and pour in the vegetable stock. Bring the pan to the boil then reduce to a simmer. Cook for approximately 35–40 minutes until the lentils are tender. Add the frozen vegetables in the last 10 minutes of cooking. Stir well then cover the pan.
5. Transfer the potatoes to a large mixing bowl. Add the vegan butter and season with salt and pepper. Using a masher or the back of a fork, mash the ingredients together until smooth.
6. Transfer the lentil filling to your baking dish and gently cover it with the mashed potato. Smooth down the potato.
7. Place the baking dish on a baking sheet, in case any of the filling overflows. Bake for approximately 10–15 minutes or until the potato has begun to brown on top.
8. Allow to cool a little then serve.

Midnight Magic (Black Bean Quinoa)

Ingredients

- 2 tbsp extra virgin olive oil
- 1 small white onion, diced
- 1 red bell pepper, diced
- 2 garlic cloves, minced
- 1 tsp chilli powder
- 1 tsp cumin
- 1 tsp dried oregano
- salt
- 150 g (5 oz) sweetcorn, drained
- 400 g (14 oz) tin black beans, drained and rinsed
- 125 g (4 oz) uncooked quinoa, rinsed
- 425 g (15 oz) passata
- 300 ml (10 fl oz) water

Makes: 4 servings
Prep Time: 10 minutes
Cook Time: 45 minutes

Method

1 Warm the oil in a large pan over a medium heat. Add the onion and cook for approximately 2–3 minutes, until translucent.

2 Stir in the pepper, garlic, spices, oregano and salt. Cook for five minutes.

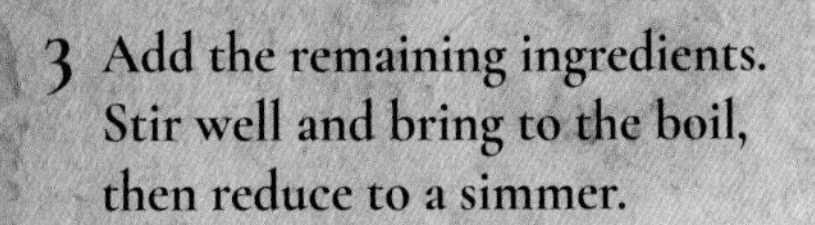

3. Add the remaining ingredients. Stir well and bring to the boil, then reduce to a simmer.
4. Cover the pan with a lid and leave to cook for approximately 30 minutes, until the quinoa has softened and most of the liquid has been absorbed. Stir occasionally.
5. Serve and enjoy on its own or with a helping of guacamole.

ENCHANTRESS (*Mushroom & Beetroot Risotto*)

INGREDIENTS

Makes: 4 to 5 servings
Prep Time: 15 minutes
Cook time: 45 minutes

- 2 tbsp olive oil
- 1 white onion, chopped
- 2 garlic cloves, minced
- 200 g (7 oz) chestnut mushrooms, sliced
- 450 g (16 oz) risotto rice
- 2 tbsp vegan white wine
- 1 ltr (35 fl oz) vegetable stock, plus extra as needed
- 270 g (10 oz) beetroot, grated
- 1 tbsp nutritional yeast
- 1 tbsp vegan butter
- salt and pepper
- 12–15 shiitake mushrooms for garnish, whole
- 2 tbsp water
- dill for garnish

Turn the page for the method.

Method

1. Heat one tablespoon of oil in a large pan over a medium heat and add the onion and garlic. Sauté for approx. 2–3 minutes until softened, then add the chestnut mushrooms and cook until browned.
2. Stir in the rice and cook until turning translucent, then pour in the vegan white wine and allow it to simmer. Continue to stir and cook until the wine has been absorbed.
3. Stir in around 100 ml (3 fl oz) of the vegetable stock. Once it's absorbed, add a little more (continue adding the stock in small amounts, leaving it to absorb before adding more). When about half the stock has been added, stir in the beetroot. Continue stirring in the stock in small amounts until it's fully absorbed and the rice is plump and tender.
4. Add the nutritional yeast and vegan butter, stirring well for a creamy texture. Season with salt and pepper.
5. Prepare the shiitake mushrooms by trimming any tough stems.
6. In a separate pan, heat the remaining tablespoon of oil over a medium heat and add the whole shiitake mushrooms. Cook them for approximately 8–10 minutes, tossing them so they become tender and both sides turn golden brown. Add two tablespoons of water and continue to toss the mushrooms until the water has evaporated.
7. Dish up the risotto and serve with the shiitake mushrooms and a sprig of dill on top.

Witches' Fingers (Spicy Okra Curry)

Ingredients

- 250 g (9 oz) okra, chopped
- 3 tbsp olive oil
- ½ tsp cumin
- 1 white onion, chopped
- 1 green chilli, chopped
- ¾ tbsp ginger garlic paste
- 2 large tomatoes, chopped and deseeded
- salt
- 1 tsp garam masala
- ½ tsp red chilli powder
- ¼ tsp turmeric
- water, as needed

Makes: 4 servings
Prep Time: 15 minutes
Cook Time: 45 to 60 minutes

Turn the page for the method.

METHOD

1. Prepare the okra by washing and draining them well, then pat them dry with a clean cloth. Chop off and discard both ends, then chop the okra into even pieces.
2. Heat 1½ tablespoons of the oil in a pan over a medium heat. Add the okra and sauté until partially cooked, for approximately 5–7 minutes, stirring often. Transfer the okra to a bowl and set aside.
3. To make the masala base, heat the remaining oil in the pan and add the cumin. Once the cumin begins to 'splutter', stir in the onion and chilli. Cook for approx. 2–3 minutes until they begin to turn golden. Add the ginger garlic paste and cook for another 2–3 minutes.
4. Add the tomatoes and a little salt. Give the masala base a good stir and cook until the tomatoes turn soft and mushy. Mix in the garam masala, red chilli powder and turmeric.
5. Pour in 60–120 ml (2–4 fl oz) water, being careful not to add too much. Taste and add a little more salt if needed. Stir then add the cooked okra. Stir again until combined.
6. Cover the pan and cook the curry on a low–medium heat until the okra is slightly tender. Once cooked, uncover the pan to allow the excess moisture to evaporate.
7. Serve with vegan paratha or rice. Enjoy!

Chocolate Poison (Chocolate Truffles)

Ingredients

- 150 g (5 oz) almonds
- 15 g (½ oz) pine nuts
- 80 g (3 oz) desiccated coconut
- 40 g (1½ oz) vegan cocoa powder, plus more for rolling
- 120 ml (4 fl oz) maple syrup

Makes: 15 truffles
Prep Time: 10 to 15 minutes
Extra Time: freeze until firm

Method

1. Line a baking tray with greaseproof paper.
2. Put the almonds into a food processor and process until finely chopped.
3. Add the pine nuts, desiccated coconut and cocoa powder. Process again to mix all the ingredients together.
4. Pour in the maple syrup while the processor is still running. Continue to process until well combined and a sticky 'dough' forms.
5. Put some cocoa powder into a small bowl, ready to roll the truffles in.
6. Roll the 'dough' between your palms to form truffle balls. Roll each ball in the cocoa powder until covered, then place the balls on the prepared baking tray.
7. Pop the tray in the freezer and leave until the truffles are firm, then tuck in.

Unicorn Blood (Chia Pudding)

Ingredients

For the chia pudding:
- 250 ml (9 fl oz) almond milk
- 4 tbsp chia seeds
- ½ tsp vanilla extract
- ½ tbsp maple syrup
- ½ tsp blue spirulina powder

For the topping:
- 400 ml (14 fl oz) tin coconut milk
- 1–2 tbsp icing sugar
- frozen blackberries
- frozen blueberries

Makes: 2 to 3 servings
Prep Time: 10 to 15 minutes
Extra Time: 24 hours

Method

1. Pop the tin of coconut milk in the fridge for 24 hours to chill before making the coconut whipped cream.
2. To make the chia pudding, add all the pudding ingredients to a bowl and mix well. Refrigerate overnight to chill.

3 To make the coconut whipped cream, scoop the solid coconut cream out of the tin and into a large mixing bowl. (Discard or save the coconut water for another recipe.)

4 Either use a standing mixer or electric hand mixer to beat the coconut cream. Beat until it's fluffy and smooth then gently fold in the icing sugar. Put the whipped cream in the fridge until ready to use.

5 It's time to assemble the pudding jars! Spoon in the chia pudding, top with the coconut whipped cream and finish with some frozen berries.

Hypnotic Love (Chocolate & Hazelnut Mousse)

Ingredients

- 115 g (4 oz) dark chocolate (at least 60% cocoa), chopped, reserve some for garnish
- 2 ripe avocados
- 3 tbsp unsweetened cocoa powder
- 60 ml (2 fl oz) unsweetened almond milk
- 1 tsp vanilla extract
- pinch of salt
- 2 tsp maple syrup
- hazelnuts for garnish, chopped
- mint for garnish

Makes: 4 servings
Prep Time: 15 to 20 minutes

Method

1. To melt the chocolate, put it in a microwave-proof bowl and heat in 15-second intervals, stirring between each burst. Be careful not to let the chocolate burn.
2. Take the chocolate out of the microwave when it's almost completely melted. Stir until it's smooth and set it aside to cool.

3. Cut the avocados in half by running a knife around them from top to bottom. Twist them in half and take out the pit. Use a spoon to remove the flesh, then discard the skin and pit. Add the flesh and the rest of the ingredients, except the hazelnuts and mint for garnish, to a blender. Blend until smooth and creamy, scraping down the sides as necessary.
4. Serve with the chopped hazelnuts and chocolate on top, finished with a sprig of mint. Indulge!